Meet Molly

Activity Book

Name _____

Age _____

Class _____

OXFORD

UNIVERSITY PRESS

OXFORD
UNIVERSITY PRESS

Great Clarendon Street, Oxford OX2 6DP

Oxford University Press is a department of the University of Oxford.
It furthers the University's objective of excellence in research, scholarship,
and education by publishing worldwide in

Oxford New York

Auckland Bangkok Buenos Aires Cape Town Chennai
Dar es Salaam Delhi Hong Kong Istanbul Karachi Kolkata
Kuala Lumpur Madrid Melbourne Mexico City Mumbai
Nairobi São Paulo Shanghai Taipei Tokyo Toronto

OXFORD and OXFORD ENGLISH are registered trade marks of
Oxford University Press in the UK and in certain other countries

ISBN: 978 0 19 440144 9

Printed in China

Activities by: Rebecca Brooke
Illustrations by: Ian Cunliffe
Original story by: Richard Northcott

Connect.

cat •

dog •

bug •

door •

dinosaur •

window •

1

2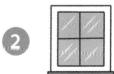

3

4

5

6

Trace and write.

 hand   hand   hand

 foot

 finger

 leg

 mouth

 eye

Circle.

❶ three fingers

❷ five fingers

❸ four fingers

❹ six fingers

Trace and connect.

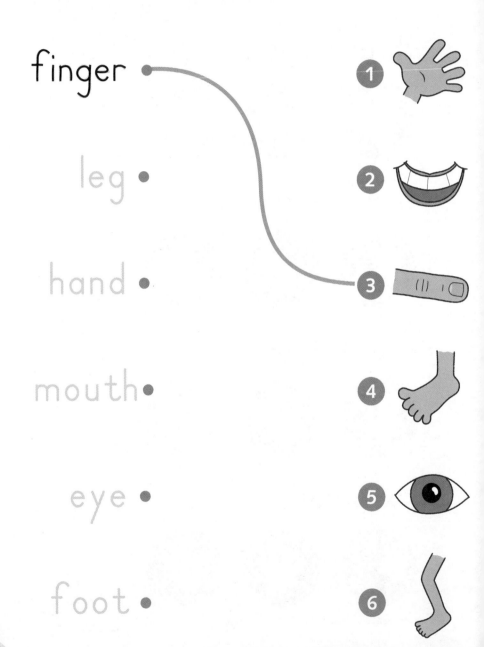

finger

leg

hand

mouth

eye

foot

Write.

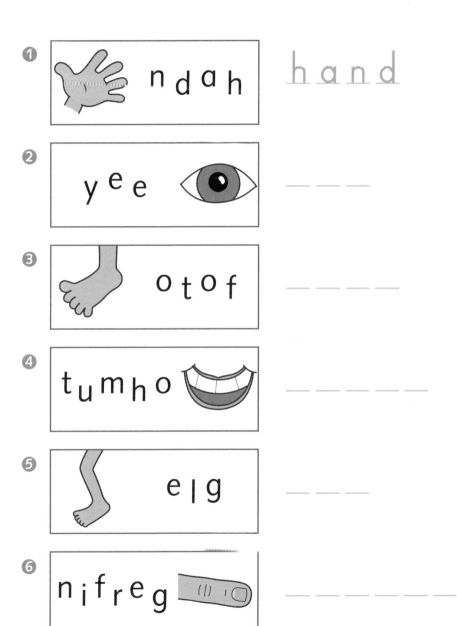

1. n d a h   hand

2. y e e

3. o t o f

4. t u m h o

5. e l g

6. n i f r e g

Circle yes or no .

1. Joe is a girl.

   yes
   (no)

2. Joe has two eyes.

   yes
   no

3. The dog is red.

   yes
   no

4. Molly does not like Joe.

   yes
   no

5. Molly is a girl.

   yes
   no

6. The dog has four legs.

   yes
   no

7. The bug has
   two mouths.

   yes
   no

Write.

shirt   Joe   shoes
Molly   pants   eyes

① Joe and __Molly__ are friends.

② Joe has blue _____.

③ _____ likes dogs.

④ Joe has green _____.

⑤ Joe has a blue _____.

⑥ Joe has white _____.

Circle yes or no .

1 Molly has green eyes.
yes
(no)

2 Molly has two feet.
yes
no

3 Molly has ten fingers.
yes
no

4 Molly has a red hat.
yes
no

5 Molly has white shoes.
yes
no

6 Molly can draw.
yes
no

What page?

1. Molly draws a door. `10`

2. Molly draws Joe.

3. Molly draws a hand.

4. Molly draws a dog.

5. Molly draws two legs.

6. Molly draws two feet.

7. Molly draws five fingers.

Write.

1 How many houses?

three

2 How many red cars?

_____

3 How many trees?

_____

4 How many windows?

_____

5 How many blue doors?

_____

6 How many black cats?

_____

Trace and connect.

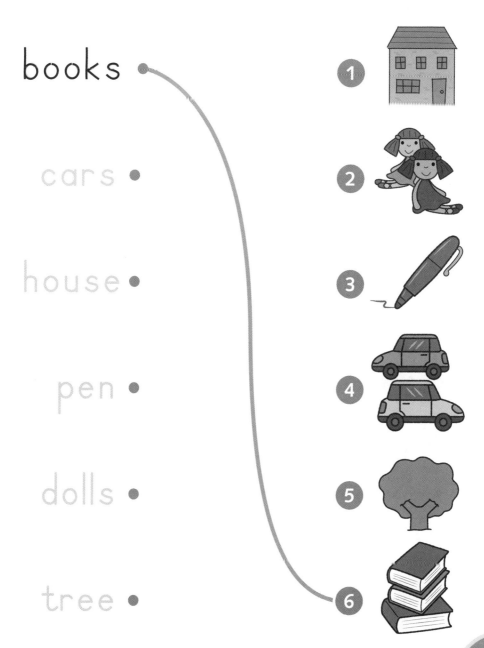

books

cars

house

pen

dolls

tree

1

2

3

4

5

6

Circle.

❶ Who likes dinosaurs?
Molly (Joe) the dog

❷ What color are Joe's eyes?
red   green   blue

❸ What color is Molly's door?
black   blue   red

❹ Who does not like doors?
Joe   the dog   the dinosaur

❺ How many legs does the
bug have? two   four   six

❻ How many eyes does the
bug have? two   four   six

Look and write.

Chant.

Molly draws a hand.
  This is her hand.
Molly draws five fingers.
  These are her fingers.
Molly draws two legs.
  These are her legs.
Molly draws two feet.
  These are her feet.
Molly draws Joe.
  He is her friend.
Molly draws a dog.
  Joe likes dogs.
Molly draws a door.
  Open the door, Joe.